THE SECRET PROJECT

WITHDRAWN

JONAH WINTER

illustrated by

JEANETTE WINTER

BEACH LANE BOOKS

New York London Toronto Sydney New Delhi

In the beginning, there was just a peaceful desert mountain landscape,

a quiet little boys' school where the boys
wore shorts and played outdoor games.

Then came a letter addressed to the principal.
It was from the United States government.
The principal was told that his school
was needed for important government work.
The boys would need to clear out.
Soon.

The boys cleared out.
The school shut down.
All was quiet.

Not long after, cars begin arriving at the shut-down school. They are carrying the most brilliant scientists in the world. From the far corners of the earth, the scientists are driven to this secret location which has no name, which does not even officially exist.

One by one, other workers are brought in—
to cook, to clean, to guard.
They are told nothing about why they've been brought here.
They are sworn to secrecy about the existence of this place.

Night and day, the greatest scientists in the world
conduct experiments and research in the laboratory.
They are working on something they call the "Gadget."
What they are trying to invent is so secret,
they cannot even call it by its real name.

Night and day, they are trying to figure out
how to take the tiniest particle in the world,
the atom,
and cut it in half, making it even tinier.

Outside the laboratory, nobody knows they are there.
Outside, there are just peaceful desert mountains
and mesas, cacti, coyotes, prairie dogs.

Outside the laboratory, in the faraway nearby,
artists are painting beautiful paintings.

Outside the laboratory, in the faraway nearby,
Hopi Indians are carving beautiful dolls out of wood
as they have done for centuries.

Meanwhile, inside the laboratory, the shadowy figures are getting closer to completing their secret invention.

The shadowy figures are making calculations that will help them create something gigantic . . . out of something tiny.
The clock is ticking.
These great scientists must complete their secret invention before any other scientists complete *their* secret invention.

Sometimes the shadowy figures emerge from the shadows, pale and tired and hollow-eyed, and go to the nearby town.

They must not tell anybody who they are,
where they are working, or what they are working on.
They smile and say, "Good day!"

When they drive back to the laboratory,
they must make sure that no one is following them.

They must pass through the security gate,
where they must show their identification.

Back in the laboratory, the shadowy figures return to their work.
They must complete their invention.
The clock is ticking.
Only a little more research is needed—

research on a metal called uranium
that can be turned into something with enormous power,
and research on a metal called plutonium,
which also can be turned into something with enormous power.

After two years of almost constant research,
the "Gadget" is completed, ready to be tested.
The great scientists gather around their creation
in silence, wondering if it will work.

Then, under the cover of darkness,
they pack the "Gadget" onto a truck
and drive off into the night.

They drive through the desert and hope no one notices.

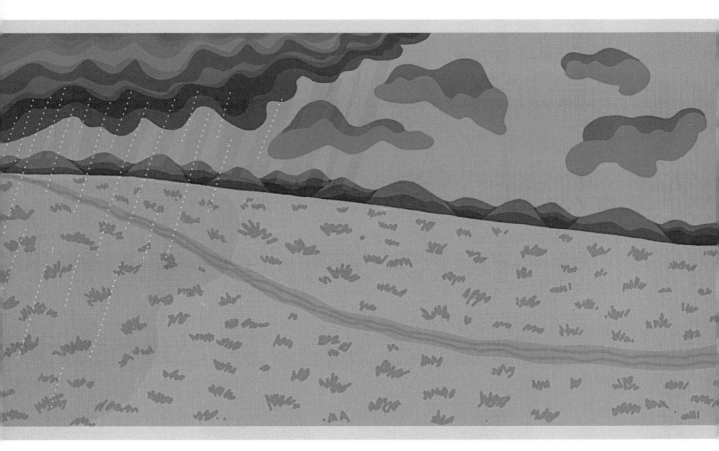

They arrive at a wide open space
that is perfect for their purposes—
just miles and miles of sand,
far from any towns.

They wheel their secret "Gadget" out to the tower.

Now they must drive to a safe distance
where they can observe their test
without getting hurt.

Crouching down in their bunker,
the scientists prepare themselves
for something so loud,
so earth-shattering,
so huge,
it is hardly even imaginable.

The countdown begins:

Ten.

Nine.

Eight.

Seven.

Six.

Five.
Four.
Three.
Two.
One . . .

AUTHOR'S NOTE

In March of 1943, the United States government started bringing nuclear physicists, chemists, and scientific researchers to a remote location in the New Mexico desert to begin work on a secret project that they referred to as the "Gadget." This remote location had no name known to the general public, but it was referred to by the government as "Site Y." (Originally, it had been the site of an elite private academy called the Los Alamos Ranch School.) It was about a 45-minute drive from Santa Fe, and the only proof of its existence was a post office box: P.O. Box 1663. A highly respected scientist named J. Robert Oppenheimer was in charge of this secret project, and he assembled the greatest scientific minds he could find from all over America and the world. Some of them were refugees from Nazi Germany. Some were Nobel Prize winners. Together, they created the first atomic bomb. And they first tested this atomic bomb on July 16, 1945, in the desert of southern New Mexico within the White Sands Missile Range, at a place they called the "Trinity" site.

The explosion was 10,000 times as hot as the sun and could be seen and felt for 160 miles. It caused windows to break 120 miles away. The mushroom cloud was about 7 miles high. In the area surrounding the explosion site, where the fireball engulfed the sand, greenish-gray glass particles formed, creating a new and highly radioactive mineral dubbed "trinitite." Dangerously high levels of plutonium were found in plants, animals, and the soil for a 100-mile radius from the explosion, and scientists estimate that this radioactivity will remain for 24,100 years. As of 2014, the United States government is finally in the process of studying the cancer caused by high radiation levels in citizens who lived in New Mexico during the test. Many people believe that such studies should have been conducted several decades ago.

For the most part, the clerks and cooks and other people who worked at Site Y had no idea what the scientists were creating. The scientists were sworn to such a deep level of secrecy that many of them had to change their names before arriving in New Mexico. Incoming and outgoing mail was inspected by the government to make sure that no one had accidentally mentioned anything about the "Gadget"—and to make sure that none of them were spies.

The reason for this secrecy, and the reason for this research and invention? The United States was at war—World War II—against Nazi Germany and Japan. There had been rumors that the Nazis were hard at work developing their own atomic weapons, and the American government wanted to invent one first—to protect American lives and to win the war.

Three weeks after the Trinity test, the United States dropped two atomic bombs. The first was dropped on Hiroshima, Japan, on August 6, 1945. The second was dropped on Nagasaki, Japan, on August 9, 1945. World War II ended shortly thereafter. It has been estimated that between 164,000 and 214,000 people died as a result of these bombs, most of them civilians, many of them children.

No other atomic bomb has been used to kill people since Hiroshima and Nagasaki. Most countries have outlawed above-ground testing of nuclear weapons—because of its catastrophic effects on the environment and on human health—and are working hard to reduce their stockpiles of such weapons. However, as of 2016, there are 15,700 nuclear weapons still in existence throughout the world.

Hopefully, some day that number will be zero.

For the peacemakers

FURTHER READING

Fermi, Rachel, Richard Rhodes, and Esther Samra. *Picturing the Bomb: Photographs from the Secret World of the Manhattan Project.* New York: Harry N. Abrams, 1995.

Groves, Leslie. "The First Nuclear Test in New Mexico." Primary resource for "Truman." *American Experience.* PBS. http://www.pbs.org/wgbh/americanexperience/features /primary-resources/truman-bombtest/

Kritensen, Hans M., and Robert S. Norris. "Status of World Nuclear Forces." *Federation of American Scientists.* 2016. http://fas.org/issues/nuclear-weapons /status-world-nuclear-forces/.

Lawrence, David. "Editorial From 1945: What Hath Man Wrought!" *U.S. News & World Report,* September 28, 2015. http://www.usnews.com/news/special-reports /the-manhattan-project/articles/2015/09/28/editorial-from-1945-what-hath-man-wrought.

Light, Michael. *100 Suns: 1945–1962.* New York: Knopf, 2003.

Maruki, Toshi. *Hiroshima No Pika.* New York: Lothrop, Lee and Shepard, 1980.

Trohan, Walter. "Bare Peace Bid U.S. Rebuffed 7 Months Ago." *Chicago Tribune,* August 19, 1945. http://archives.chicagotribune.com/1945/08/19/page/1/article /bare-peace-bid-u-s-rebuffed-7-months-ago.

Wellerstein, Alex. "The First Light of Trinity." *New Yorker,* July 16, 2015. http://www .newyorker.com/tech/elements/the-first-light-of-the-trinity-atomic-test.

BEACH LANE BOOKS An imprint of Simon & Schuster Children's Publishing Division • 1230 Avenue of the Americas, New York, New York 10020 • Text copyright © 2017 by Jonah Winter • Illustrations copyright © 2017 by Jeanette Winter • All rights reserved, including the right of reproduction in whole or in part in any form. • BEACH LANE BOOKS is a trademark of Simon & Schuster, Inc. • For information about special discounts for bulk purchases, please contact Simon & Schuster Special Sales at 1-866-506-1949 or business@simonandschuster .com. • The Simon & Schuster Speakers Bureau can bring authors to your live event. For more information or to book an event, contact the Simon & Schuster Speakers Bureau at 1-866-248-3049 or visit our website at www.simonspeakers.com. • Book design by Ann Bobco • The text for this book was set in Neutraface. • Manufactured in China • 1116 SCP • First Edition • 10 9 8 7 6 5 4 3 2 1 • Library of Congress Cataloging-in-Publication Data • Names: Winter, Jonah, 1962- author. | Winter, Jeanette, illustrator. • Title: The secret project / Jonah Winter ; illustrated by Jeanette Winter. • Description: First edition. | New York : Beach Lane Books, [2017] | • Includes bibliographical references. • Identifiers: LCCN 2016018832| ISBN 9781481469135 (hardcover : alk. paper)| ISBN 9781481469142 (e-book)